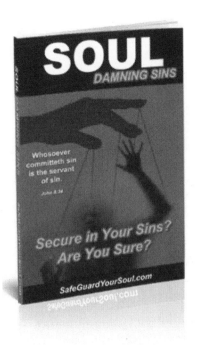

Soul Damning Sins

Victory in the Power of the Holy Ghost!

SafeGuardYourSoul.com

Soul Damning Sins

ISBN-13: 978-1475043983

SafeGuardYourSoul.com
Frisco, Texas
Visit www.SafeGuardYourSoul.com

ISBN-13: 978-1475043983

Printed in the United States of America

All Scripture quotations deliberately taken from the Authorized Version of the Holy Bible, the King James Version

Cover Design by Bill Wegener at
colorenlargement.com.

Do you desire to learn God's Word? – To begin receiving the *Moments with My Master* email that is sent out 2-3 times weekly, go to SafeGuardYourSoul.com and sign up. Or, email info@safeguardyoursoul.com.

Forward by Stephen Michels

"Every time I read these words, my heart is convicted to pursue holiness and Jesus at all costs! This information is from the heart of God and all souls who want to be with Him in His house must know what He requires so there will be no self-deception in our lives. We need to keep speaking the truth. This is critical knowledge and it is urgently needed now if we are to understand the full-counsel of God and be prepared to meet Christ, escaping the fires of eternal damnation." Stephen Michels

Introduction

It is by no accident – actually by divine design – that there are several lists of soul-damning sins in the New Testament canon. These lists are a vital component of God's Word and must not be neglected by the true disciple of Jesus. Although most who miss-lead others purposely evade this lists of sins, they are clearly identified and written in Holy Scripture by divine ordination. They must be studied and learned by every honest student of God's Word (Luke 8:15). Perhaps these sins are a litmus test to reveal just how true (or untrue) our walk with God is (or is not). That noble hearted disciple, who desires to be preserved unto eternal life, will allow the fear of the LORD to invade his heart, being broken and contrite, while falling afresh upon the mercy of God in repentance. The foolish heart will pass on by, refusing to prepare himself, and find himself soon hearing the most horrible words of rejection to ever enter human ear – **"Depart from me, ye cursed, into everlasting fire, prepared for the devil and his angels."** (Matthew 25:41)

This litmus test is a warning and a gift of divine mercy. "Everlasting fire" was not originally created for men, but rather "prepared for the devil and his angels." By this, we deduce that God does not want any human soul going to this domain of the damned. This is why He gave us His only begotten Son (John 3:16).

Do you remember back in school when the teacher would give you a trial test that didn't count for your grade, yet it revealed just where you were or weren't in your understanding of the subject? If you were like me, you realized just how much catching up you had to do, and that the trial run test helped you to realize you were not ready to take the final test and would fail if you did not immediately prepare.

SOUL-DAMNING SINS

Are Your Sins Worth Your Eternal Soul?

"What Shall a Man Give in Exchange for His Soul?"
Mark 8:37

Table of Contents

SafeGuardYourSoul.com

Chapter One

Are there Certain Sins that will Damn the Soul?

If there were a list of deadly sins, which are sure to damn your soul to eternal hell, would you want to know about that list?

Because of His abundant mercy, lists of specific sins that provoke the LORD to anger are listed in His Word. This is in order to warn men and bless them to escape His sure judgment to come on those who walk in such rebellion.

"Now the works of the flesh are manifest, which are THESE; <u>Adultery</u>, <u>fornication</u>, <u>uncleanness</u>, <u>lasciviousness</u>, <u>Idolatry</u>, <u>witchcraft</u>, <u>hatred</u>, <u>variance</u>, <u>emulations</u>, <u>wrath</u>, <u>strife</u>, <u>seditions</u>, <u>heresies</u>, <u>Envyings</u>, <u>murders</u>, <u>drunkenness</u>, <u>revellings</u>, and such like: of the which I tell you before, as I have also told you in time past, that <u>they which do such things SHALL NOT inherit the kingdom of God</u>." Galatians 5:19-21

Let's observe a brief definition of the 17 manifestations of the sinful nature listed here in Galatians 5:19-21 – a much neglected text:

- **"Adultery"** –looking on another to lust (in person or via technology); unlawful relations involving a married person. Adultery is defined in Scripture as any sex involving the heart and/or body that is outside of holy matrimony where God designed it to be enjoyed between one man and one woman (Matthew 5:28; Hebrews 13:4).

- **"Fornication"** – every and all forms of illicit sexual activity, whether in thought or deed. Any sexual activity outside of holy matrimony. This includes any type of pornographic involvement.

- **"Uncleanness"** – anything opposite of purity; all forms of sexual impurity.

- **"Lasciviousness"** – licentiousness, lust, lewdness, unchastity. Anything promoting or inciting sexual lust; lack of restraint.

- **"Idolatry"** – image worship. This includes anything other than the LORD upon which the affections are passionately set.

- **"Witchcraft"** – sorcery. The practice of dealing with evil spirits, magical incantations, casting spells or charms by means of drugs or potions to inflict harm on another. Witch-craft includes the evil manipulation or control of others by any means.

- **"Hatred"** – enmity, bitter dislike, malice, abhorrence; tendency to hold grudges against or be angry with another.

- **"Variance"** – discord, dissentions, quarrelling, debating and disputes.

- **"Emulations"** – striving to excel at the expense of another person; seeking to surpass or outdo another.

- **"Wrath"** – rage; determined enduring anger; fierce indignation with turbulent passions.

- **"Strife"** – disputations, strife about words, angry contentions; vindictive endeavor to repay another evil for evil.

- **"Seditions"** – parties, factions; stirring up strife among people.

- **"Heresies"** – the rejection of truth for fallacy; departure from divinely revealed truth.

- **"Envyings"** – ill will toward another's good fortune.

- **"Murders"** – to kill or mar the happiness of another.

- **"Drunkenness"** – intoxication from the over-use of alcohol.

- **"Revellings"** – rioting; lascivious and bois-terous feastings including obscene music and other sinful activities; carousing.

These are the exact soul-damning **"works of the flesh"** the apostle Paul speaks of in this same passage when he declares that **"they that are Christ's have crucified the flesh with the affections and lusts."** (Galatians 5:19, 24)

Any person who currently has any one of these sins in their lives, is not presently submitted to Christ and is in danger of eternal hell fire.

Regretfully, in this hour of great apostasy, scarcely do we hear leaders tend to this divinely inspired biblical doctrine. We were often warned by Christ and His apostles that in these last days "**many false prophets**" will "**deceive many.**" (Matthew 7:15; 24:3-5, 11, 24; 1 John 4:1).

Jesus is **"that great shepherd of the sheep"** and desires to bring each of those He has saved home safely for eternity (John 10:1-18; Hebrews 13:20). The Bible reveals to us that **"God is love"** and that He **"is longsuffering to usward, not willing that any should perish, but that all should come to repentance."** (2 Peter 3:9)

"As I live, saith the Lord GOD, I have no pleasure in the death of the wicked; but that the wicked turn from his way and live: turn ye, turn ye from your evil ways; for why will ye die, O house of Israel?" Ezekiel 33:11

The LORD's desire to keep and protect those

whom He saved is the reason for the many warnings He put in His Word. Why then is this vital part of the Bible intentionally avoided by so many in leadership today? It's because so many pastors and leaders today teach the diabolical lie of "once saved always saved" which is never found in God's Word in concept or in wording.

Does your pastor or favorite author teach this lie? The Bible forewarned us that in the final days, **"ungodly men"** would pervert the grace of God by making it out to be a license for sin. When we see some teaching this falsehood, we can see that the fruit of their doctrine if false. Beware! This teaching is one way to detect a false leader.

"Beloved, when I gave all diligence to write unto you of the common salvation, it was needful for me to write unto you, and exhort you that ye should earnestly contend for the faith which was once delivered unto the saints. For there are certain men crept in

unawares, who were before of old ordained to this condemnation, <u>ungodly men</u>, <u>turning the grace of our God into lasciviousness (license for sin)</u>, and denying the only Lord God, and our Lord Jesus Christ." Jude 3-4

The Son of God warned:

"Beware of false prophets, which come to you in sheep's clothing, but inwardly they are ravening wolves." Matthew 7:15

Chapter Two

The Written Word of God
is the Final Authority

"Heaven and earth shall pass away: but my words shall not pass away." Mark 13:31

Jesus tells us here that His Word will never change as He will never change (Malachi 3:6). No mere man is above God's Law/Word and so beware of any many who speaks contrary to what is revealed to us in God's Word (Isaiah

8:20).

Concerning the divine inspiration of the Word of God and the propensity of many to twist it to their own liking, pastor and author pastor Mark Case writes:

"It is impossible for Truth to contradict itself, thus there are no contradictions in the Word of God. However, the appearance of contradictions based strictly on 'the letter' give opportunities for deceivers to invent unfounded theological questions. Deceitful religious men reduce God's divine, spiritual truths to a humanly intellectual argument, then pretend to decipher the curiosities they created. Their conclusions form deceptive religious doctrines that sabotage the understanding of the masses who are in pursuit of God's will. Such was the case with the formulation of John Calvin's 'Five Points' and also that which is known as 'eternal security,' and such is the case with the masses who pursue God today.

Now for the truth about this matter: From the beginning of the Bible to the end, the Bible story clearly illustrates that it is only through a continual pursuit of God's righteousness that we can have absolute confidence of salvation through the righteousness freely given by Jesus Christ. To believe on Jesus Christ for salvation is to pursue the righteousness of God just as He did. While the merit for our salvation is based strictly upon the merit of the righteousness of Jesus Christ, the Bible does make abundantly clear that there is a divine relationship between His righteousness freely given, and our daily walk in that righteousness. Believer beware! To those 'that work iniquity,' He will say, 'Depart from Me.' (Matt. 7:21)" Mark Case, Proclaim-It.org

As Mark Case points out, the lawless will not inherit eternal glory, regardless of what past relationship they may have had with Christ. Those who know Christ walk with Him in intimate fellowship and obey Him.

"He that saith, I know him, and keepeth not his commandments, is a liar, and the truth is not in him." 1 John 2:4

Divine Truth is Unchanging

"For ever, O LORD, thy word is settled in heaven." Psalm 119:89

The truth concerning the Bible revelation of a *conditional* eternal salvation, upsets some and so they err into emotions or tradition instead of holding to the Word of God stringently.

The Bible tells us that God has magnified His Word above even His very name! (Psalms 138:2) Those who truly serve Him, magnify His Words and not those of mere men or contrary doctrines. The mark of a true disciple will be that he searches out and magnifies God's written Word above all else and allows it to supersede the voice, notion, persuasions, or teachings of all others (Psalm 138:2; John 5:39; 8:47; Acts 17:11).

Jesus simply says **"follow me."** (Matthew 9:9; Luke 5:27) So Jesus never told us to follow a mere man or organization of mere men. He never told any soul to follow any human being and He gave us His written Word so that we can follow Him according to His exact will and on His terms. This is why we must know His Word individually. Paul the apostle of Jesus wrote:

"Study to shew thyself approved unto God, a workman that needeth not to be ashamed, rightly dividing the word of truth." 2 Timothy 2:15

Those who do not choose to spend their days loving God more than self, will not be with Him eternally.

"My people are destroyed for lack of knowledge: because thou hast rejected knowledge, I will also reject thee, that thou shalt be no priest to me: seeing thou hast forgotten the law of thy God, I will also forget thy children." Hosea 4:6

Hell is full of people who got saved but then chose not to continue abiding in Christ and trusted their pastor or some other mere human leader instead of being submitted fully to the LORD who gave us His Word in order to follow Him on His terms (Psalms 119:104-105).

"The grass withereth, the flower fadeth: but <u>the word of our God shall stand for ever</u>." Isaiah 40:8

God gave us His Word so we could truly walk with Him and not be led astray.

"And that from a child thou hast known the holy scriptures, which are able to make thee wise unto salvation through faith which is in Christ Jesus. All scripture is given by inspiration of God, and is profitable for doctrine, for reproof, for correction, for instruction in righteousness: That the man of God may be perfect, throughly furnished unto all good works." 2 Timothy 3:15-17

Chapter Three

Sins that Defile a Man

"And he said, That which cometh out of the man, <u>that defileth the man</u>. For from within, out of the heart of men, proceed <u>evil thoughts</u>, <u>adulteries</u>, <u>fornications</u>, <u>murders</u>, <u>Thefts</u>, <u>covetousness</u>, <u>wickedness</u>, <u>deceit</u>, <u>lasciviousness</u>, <u>an evil eye</u>, <u>blasphemy</u>, <u>pride</u>, <u>foolishness</u>: All these evil things come from within, and <u>defile the man</u>." Mark 7:20-23

"Defile" refers to being unclean in the eyes of God. Jesus was speaking of *all* men here – Those whom He saves are included. He made no distinction. Those whom Jesus saves have no license to live in sin but rather have been granted saving grace to live holy as He is holy and if they don't, they will spend eternity in hell with all those who die in sin (Titus 2:11-14; Hebrews 12:14; 1 Peter 1:15-16; Revelation 21:8, 27). The proof-less, fairy tale myth of "once saved always saved" is designed to damn the souls of men and it is doing its epidemic work today. If God is **"Holy, holy, holy"** and He tells us that certain sins **"defile the man,"** it should be more than obvious that no defiled man is ready to meet Him who is Holy (Isaiah 6:3; Revelation 4:8). In fact, the Bible tells us exactly why Jesus came to the earth the first time and the exact people that Christ will return for.

"...Christ also loved the church, and gave himself for it; That he might sanctify and cleanse it with the washing of water by

the word, That he might present it to himself <u>a glorious church</u>, <u>not having spot, or wrinkle, or any such thing; but that it should be holy and without blem-ish</u>." Ephesians 5:25-27

Make no mistake: Only the LORD can make a man holy and He only makes holy (sets apart) those who truly trust in Him and obey Him. All others do not possess saving faith (1 Jn. 2:3-5; James 2; Heb. 12:14).

The Bible clearly tells us that the LORD Jesus is coming back for His **"little flock,"** a pure and spotless Bride, one washed in His holy blood according to His holy Word (Lk. 12:32; Eph. 5:25-27; Tit. 2:13-14; 1 Jn. 3:3; Rev. 2-3).

After being washed initially (born again), the re-cipient of Christ must continue to walk with Him in the light of His holy truth in order to continue to be made clean in His holy eyes and not defiled:

"But IF we walk in the light, as he is in the

light, we have fellowship one with another, and the blood of Jesus Christ his Son cleanseth us from all sin." 1 John 1:7

Any honest Bible student knows that the LORD is **"Holy, holy, holy,"** and therefore washings, holiness, and purification are of the utmost importance in the divine economy. All those who will be with Him eternally must be made holy by His grace which requires their own faith and participation - both initially and to the end of their lives in this sinful world (Num. 19; Matt. 5:8; 10:22; 24:13; 2 Cor. 7:1; Eph. 5:26-27; Tit. 1:15; Rev. 6:11; 7:9, 13).

Chapter Four

False Prophets and
the Return of Jesus

We are repeatedly warned of false leaders by our LORD and how that they will lead multitudes to eternal damnation.

"And Jesus answered and said unto them, <u>Take heed that no man deceive you</u>. For many shall come in my name, saying, I am Christ; and shall deceive many. ... And <u>many</u>

false prophets shall rise, and shall deceive many. And because iniquity (sinfulness) shall abound (be everywhere), the love of many shall wax cold. **But he that shall endure unto the end, the same shall be saved**." **Matthew 24:4-5, 10-13**

Just exactly as the Bible promised, the church world today is swamped with false leaders. How do we know who is false? Well, we know them by the fruit of their doctrine. Above we saw that Jesus says that to be saved into Heaven ultimately, one must escape the abounding sinfulness of this fallen world and to "**endure to the end.**" What Jesus told us is the opposite of the unconditional "once saved always saved" falsehood we are told by so many today.

"Many" Deceived and "Few" Saved

"Enter ye in at the strait gate: for wide is the gate, and broad is the way, that leadeth to destruction, and <u>many</u> there be which go in thereat: Because strait is the gate, and

narrow is the way, which leadeth unto life, and <u>few</u> there be that find it. Beware of false prophets, which come to you in sheep's clothing, but inwardly they are ravening wolves. Ye shall know them by their fruits. Do men gather grapes of thorns, or figs of thistles?" Matthew 7:13-16

False prophets are known by what they preach. Their doctrine is largely what their **"fruit"** is that we are to **"know them by."**

The message of the many wolves who occupy leadership positions is that their **"false Christ"** is coming back to accept a people who are not abiding in Christ and therefore are spotted by sin and love this fallen world system (Matt. 24:24; James 1:27; 1 Jn. 2:15-17). Beguilers intentionally shun, downplay, and dodge away from certain passages in God's Word. They are detected to be false because they do not teach the full Counsel of God's Word. They teach people that the LORD doesn't require them to be wholly set apart but that He will accept them as they are, even if they are living in sin. According to 1 John 2:24-3:3, the remnant disciple who knows and truly loves the LORD Jesus, **"purifieth himself, even as he is pure."** Jesus' true people are known by their diligence in making themselves ready to meet Him at His soon coming.

"Let us be glad and rejoice, and give honour to him: for the marriage of the Lamb is come, and <u>his wife hath made herself ready</u>." Revelation 19:7

Chapter Five

Why Did Jesus Come to the Earth?

"And she shall bring forth a son, and thou shalt call his name JESUS: for <u>he shall save his people from their sins</u>." Matthew 1:21

Why did the Son of God give Himself on the cross? Who is He going to soon return for? God told us the answers to these vital questions plainly in His Word:

"Looking for that blessed hope, and the

glorious appearing of the great God and our Saviour Jesus Christ; <u>Who gave himself for us, that he might redeem us from all iniquity, and purify unto himself a peculiar people, zealous of good works</u>. These things speak, and exhort, and rebuke with all authority. Let no man despise thee." Titus 2:13-15

Jesus came to purchase and to **"purify unto himself a peculiar (special) people, zealous of good works"** and will soon appear for those who are abiding in Him and therefore allowing Him to purify their lives from that which defiles. The backslider simply will not be ready when Jesus returns (Matt. 25:1-13; Lk. 21:34-36). If one refuses to repent and keep his relationship with the LORD current, God will not bring him to His holy Heaven at the rapture nor in the end of his life (whichever comes first). He often warned His people concerning being ready to enter His eternal abode.

If Heaven were a sure thing for all believers no

matter what they chose to do after being saved, why would the Holy Spirit of God have inspired Peter to warn His people concerning the eternal kingdom?

"Seeing then that all these things shall be dissolved, what manner of persons ought ye to be in all <u>holy</u> conversation and god-liness, Looking for and hasting unto the coming of the day of God, wherein the heavens being on fire shall be dissolved, and the elements shall melt with fervent heat? Nevertheless we, according to his promise, look for new heavens and a new earth, wherein dwelleth righteousness. <u>Wherefore, beloved, seeing that ye look for such things, be diligent that ye may be found of him in peace, without spot, and blameless</u>." 2 Peter 3:11-14

It is crystal clear here that being **"found of him in peace, without spot, and blameless"** is essential to spending eternity with the LORD.

It is not God's will for even one of His children to go astray yet He allows it (Luke 15). The Bible poses this question to **"holy brethren"**: **"How shall we escape (God's judgment), IF we neglect so great salvation?"** (Heb. 3:1; 2:3) By this question specifically to God's own people alone, we know that *it is possible* for those once saved to **"neglect"** God's salvation and be heading for the wrath of the Almighty. The Bible tells us here that **"IF"** we **"neglect"** His **"great salvation,"** we **"shall not escape"** His judgment. God is not going to force anyone into Heaven against their own will and He will certainly not violate His eternal, holy standard. What OSAS teachers refuse to acknowledge is that God is holy. In fact, they defy Him by minimizing or even completely ignoring His holiness. They will acknowledge that God is holy if asked, but not in their teaching or practice. It is clear that their doctrines cater to and are formed around serving themselves and not the Savior. The proof-less OSAS myth they teach propagates an utter contradiction and mockery of the holiness of God. See Hebrews 2:1-4; 10:26-39. Personal holiness is a divine prerequisite for eternal life. Without it, no man shall see the LORD (Matt. 5:8; Heb. 12:14).

SafeGuardYourSoul.com

Chapter Six

"Be Not Deceived"

The Bible clearly tells us that if one is not in the state of holiness through intimate relationship with Christ (abiding fellowship), that person simply will not go to God's holy Heaven when he leaves the earth, whether that be in the catching away or upon death, which ever comes first.

Many ask a valid question that the Holy Scriptures answer and here it is: *"Are there certain sins, which disqualify a person from Heaven? Are there sins that will damn the soul to hell? If so, which sins are they are and says who?"*

"Know ye not that the unrighteous shall not inherit the kingdom of God? BE NOT DE-CEIVED: neither <u>fornicators</u>, nor <u>idolaters</u>, nor <u>adulterers</u>, nor <u>effeminate</u>, nor <u>abusers of themselves with mankind</u> (homosexuals), Nor <u>thieves</u>, nor <u>covetous</u>, nor <u>drunkards</u>, nor <u>revilers</u>, nor <u>extortioners</u>, shall inherit the kingdom of God." 1 Corinthians 6:9-10

Did you see the 10 sins listed here which will exclude any person living in them from **"inherit (ing) the kingdom of God"**?

According to 1 Corinthians 6:9-10, here are those souls who the eternal Judge and LORD says will not **"inherit the kingdom of God"**:

- **"Fornicators"**

- **"Idolaters"**

- **"Adulterers"**

- **"Effeminate"**

- **"Abusers of themselves with mankind"** (homosexuals)

- **"Thieves"**

- **"Covetous"**

- **"Drunkards"**

- **"Revilers"**

- **"Extortioners"**

Overcoming these sins cannot be accomplished by self-effort and soul power.

"This I say then, Walk in the Spirit, and ye shall not fulfill the lust of the flesh." Galatians 5:16

Again, the question: *Do certain sins ("sins unto death"; Rom. 6:16; 1 John 5:16) disqualify a person who was once saved in grace, from Heaven/*

eternal life, if he doesn't repent?

To all men, the LORD warns:

"But the <u>fearful</u> (moral cowards, men pleasers), and <u>unbelieving</u>, and the <u>abominable</u>, and <u>murderers</u>, and <u>whoremongers</u>, and <u>sorcerers</u>, and <u>idolaters</u>, and <u>all liars</u>, shall have their part in the lake which burneth with fire and brimstone: which is the second death." Revelation 21:8

This Bible passage contains yet another list of those the LORD tells us **"shall have their part in the lake which burneth with fire and brimstone":**

- **"Fearful"** (spiritual cowards, men pleasers)

- **"Unbelieving"**

- **"Abominable"**

- **"Murderers"**

- **"Whoremongers"**

- **"Sorcerers"**

- **"Idolaters"**

- **"All liars"**

Revelation 21:8 lists eight soul-damning sins. These divinely inspired laborious lists beg the following question: *Why does God take so much time and effort to give several detailed lists of these sins to His very own people? If it only required one to "believe" and be saved at one moment in one's life and he was eternally secure regardless of what he did after that one magic moment of faith, then why the specific list?*

Are these lists not warnings?

Listen to what Jesus said to warn His own people:

"And take heed to yourselves (personal responsibility), lest at any time your hearts be overcharged (weighed down) with surfeiting (over indulgence), and drunkenness, and cares of this life, and so that day come upon

you unawares. For as a snare shall it come on all them that dwell on the face of the whole earth. Watch ye therefore, and pray always, that ye may be accounted worthy to escape all these things that shall come to pass, and to stand before the Son of man." Luke 21:34-36

Notice the specific sins Jesus warns us to not be defiled by:

- **"surfeiting"** (over indulgence)

- **"drunkenness"**

- **"cares of this life"**

The LORD gave us the specific instructions as to how to overcome:

"Watch ye therefore, and pray always, that ye may be accounted worthy to escape all these things that shall come to pass, and to stand before the Son of man." Luke 21:36

Further, the Savior says:

"Watch and pray, that ye enter not into temptation: the spirit indeed is willing, but the flesh is weak." Matthew 26:41

Diligently watching and praying is essential to remaining in fellowship with the LORD.

"But Christ as a son over his own house; whose house we are, IF WE HOLD FAST THE CONFIDENCE and the rejoicing of the hope FIRM UNTO THE END." Hebrews 3:6

It is essential to remain in fellowship with Christ after He saves us.

Chapter Seven

5 Sins that Will Keep
You Out of Heaven

**"But your iniquities have separated between you and your God, and your sins have hid his face from you, that he will not hear."
Isaiah 59:2**

Living in sin will keep us out of God's kingdom. Living in sin instead of obedience to Christ, demonstrates that we love self and sin more than the LORD (Matthew 22:37; Romans 6:16).

God's Word tells us what exact five sins kept Israel (God's covenant people) out of their promise land of blessings. These same sins are given to all New Testament believers to warn us.

"But I keep (perpetually) under my body, and bring *it* into subjection: lest that by any means, when I have preached to others, I myself should be a castaway. Moreover, brethren, I would not that ye should be ignorant, how that all our fathers were under the cloud, and all passed through the sea; And were all baptized unto Moses in the cloud and in the sea; (represents salvation) And did all eat the same spiritual meat; And did all drink the same spiritual drink: for they drank of that spiritual Rock that followed them: and that Rock was Christ. However, with many of them God was not well pleased: for they were overthrown in the wilderness. Now these things were OUR exam-

ples, to the intent we should not **LUST** after evil things, as they also lusted. Neither be ye **IDOLATERS**, as *were* some of them; as it is written, The people sat down to eat and drink, and rose up to play. Neither let us commit **FORNICATION**, as some of them committed, and fell in one day three and twenty thousand. Neither let us **TEMPT** Christ, as some of them also tempted, and were destroyed of serpents. Neither **MUR-MUR** ye, as some of them also murmured, and were destroyed of the destroyer. Now all these things happened unto them for ensamples: and they are written for our admonition, upon whom the ends of the world are come. Wherefore let him that thinketh he standeth take heed lest he fall." 1 Corinthians 9:27; 10:1-12

Drawing directly from the warning to New Testament believers above, here are the five sins that kept God's people out of their promised land:

- **"Lust"**

- **"Idolatry"**

- **"Fornication"**

- **"Tempting Christ"**

- **"Murmuring"**

For the sake of remembrance, let us use the acronym L.I.F.T.M. here. Each letter corresponds to one of these five deadly sins, which disqualify the people of the LORD from entering into His resting place – ultimately Heaven.

This simple acronym should help us to remember these sins and remain separate from these things which displease the LORD. May He bless and quicken our hearts today to cry out to Him to increase as we decrease and to grant us **"the spirit of holiness."** (Rom. 1:4; Jn. 3:30)

We need to L.I.F.T.M. up (these sins) to the LORD in repentance and for His perfect forgiveness and cleansing, submitting ourselves afresh to Him who alone is worthy. God the Holy Spirit warns us here through Paul's pen, that Israel and these sins are our **"examples."** (1 Cor. 10:6, 11) Israel fell by these exact sins and such is given to us as a striking warning. The clear message here is that God is a holy Judge and destroys those of His who depart from abiding in His presence and go back into sinfulness (transgressors – Psalms 68:21; 73:28; 125:5, etc.). *If we do not trust Christ enough to see these sins rooted out of our lives, any one of these five sins WILL keep us out of our heavenly promised land.* God is holy.

"But as he which hath called you is holy, so be ye holy in all manner of conversation; 16 Because it is written, Be ye holy; for I am holy." 1 Peter 1:15-16

Chapter Eight

No Holiness, No Heaven

Though most pastors refuse to teach such, there are many, many warnings in the New Testament Scriptures. Here's a severe warning concerning the point of no return for those who continue in their sin:

"Follow peace with all men, and <u>holiness, without which no man shall see the Lord</u>:

<u>Looking diligently lest any man fail of the grace of God</u>; lest any root of bitterness springing up trouble you, and thereby many be defiled; Heb 12:16 Lest there be any fornicator, or profane person, as Esau, who for one morsel of meat sold his birthright. For ye know how that afterward, when he would have inherited the blessing, he was rejected: for he found no place of repentance, though he sought it carefully with tears." Hebrews 12:14-17

Crying out to the LORD is a good thing. David did so many times as we have on record in the book of Psalms.

"For they that are after the flesh do mind the things of the flesh; but they that are after the Spirit the things of the Spirit. For to be carnally minded *is* death; but to be spiritually minded *is* life and peace." Romans 8:5-6

It simply does not matter how sincere someone

is or how sure they may feel that they are saved and going to Heaven. If that person is not saved *from* sin, they are not saved *for* Heaven. Living in sin clearly testifies that a person is not right with Him who is "**Holy, holy, holy**" and will have no part with Him in eternity (Isa. 6:3; Rev. 4:8).

"And every man that hath this hope in him purifieth himself, even as he is pure. Whosoever committeth sin transgresseth also the law: for sin is the transgression of the law. And ye know that he was manifested to take away our sins; and in him is no sin. Whosoever abideth in him sinneth not: whosoever sinneth hath not seen him, neither known him. Little children, let no man deceive you: he that doeth righteousness is righteous, even as he is righteous. He that committeth sin is of the devil; for the devil sinneth from the beginning. For this purpose the Son of God was manifested, that he might destroy the works of the devil. Whoso-

ever is born of God doth not commit sin; for his seed remaineth in him: and he cannot sin, because he is born of God. In this the children of God are manifest, and the children of the devil: whosoever doeth not righteousness is not of God, neither he that loveth not his brother." 1 John 3:3-10

Chapter Nine

"Fleshly Lusts Which War Against the Soul"

"Mortify therefore your members which are upon the earth; fornication, uncleanness, inordinate affection, evil concupiscence, and covetousness, which is idolatry: For which things' sake the wrath of God cometh on the children of disobedience: In the which ye al-

SafeGuardYourSoul.com

so walked some time, when ye lived in them.
But now ye also put off all these; anger,
wrath, malice, blasphemy, filthy communi-
cation out of your mouth. Lie not one to another, seeing that ye have put off the old
man with his deeds." Colossians 3:5-9

Here in Colossians 3, the Word informs us that
there are six sins **"For which things' sake the
wrath of God cometh on the children of disobedience."**

- **"Fornication"**

- **"Uncleanness"**

- **"Inordinate affection"** (exceeding reasona-
  ble limits, excessive)

- **"Evil concupiscence"** (secret desire for that
  which is forbidden, i.e., fantasies, fantasiz-
  ing of sinful activities)

- **"Covetousness"**

     "Idolatry"

Ephesians 5:

"For this ye know, that no whoremonger, nor unclean person, nor covetous man, who is an idolater, hath any inheritance in the kingdom of Christ and of God. Let no man deceive you with vain words: for because of these things cometh the wrath of God upon the children of disobedience." Ephesians 5:5 -6

Notice that after the Holy Spirit here lists four violations against the holiness of God (sins), He says: **"Let no man deceive you with vain words: for because of <u>these things</u> cometh the wrath of God upon the children of disobedience."** (Ephesians 5:6)

- **"Whoremonger"**

- **"Unclean person"**

- **"Covetous man"**

- **"Idolater"**

He tells us here that no person who is living outside of fellowship with the LORD and therefore committing these sins, **"hath any inheritance in the kingdom of Christ and of God"** and to **"Let no man deceive you with vain words: for because of these things (these sins named) cometh the wrath of God upon the children of disobedience."** (Ephesians 5:5 -6)

Here as in other places, the apostle is warning believers to never be deceived into thinking that any person practicing these sins has an inheritance in the eternal kingdom of God. Saint of the LORD, here in this passage, the Holy Spirit instructs us to never allow any leader to seduce our hearts and convince our minds that sin does not endanger the eternal soul.

"Dearly beloved, I beseech *you* as strangers and pilgrims, <u>abstain from fleshly lusts, which war against the soul</u>." 1 Peter 2:11

Living in temporal sin endangers the eternal soul.

Chapter Ten

The 7 Deadly Sins

Here are seven the deadly sins of Proverbs 6:

"These six *things* doth the LORD hate: yea, seven *are* an abomination unto him: A proud look, a lying tongue, and hands that shed innocent blood, An heart that deviseth wicked imaginations, feet that be swift in running to mischief, A false witness *that* speaketh

lies, and he that soweth discord among brethren." Proverbs 6:16-19

- "A proud look"

- "A lying tongue"

- "Hands that shed innocent blood"

- "An heart that deviseth wicked imaginations"

- "Feet that be swift in running to mischief"

- "A false witness *that* speaketh lies"

- "He that soweth discord among brethren"

"Having therefore these promises, dearly beloved, <u>let us cleanse ourselves from all filthiness of the flesh and spirit, perfecting holiness in the fear of God</u>." 2 Corinthians 7:1

"Therefore I will judge you, O house of Israel, every one according to his ways, saith the Lord GOD. <u>Repent, and turn *yourselves* from all your transgressions; so iniquity shall not be your ruin</u>. Cast away from you all your transgressions, whereby ye have transgressed; and make you a new heart and a new spirit: for why will ye die, O house of Israel? For I have no pleasure in the death of him that dieth, saith the Lord GOD: wherefore turn *yourselves*, and live ye." Ezekiel 18:30-32

"That which is altogether just shalt thou follow, that thou mayest live, and inherit the land which the LORD thy God giveth thee." Deuteronomy 16:20

The LORD told us that there would be those who professed to know Him and yet by their works they deny Him. These **"works of the flesh"** which we have studied here are not according to Christ. They are not the character of Jesus and reveal a life that is not conformed to His holy image (Rom. 8:29). These characteristics should never be manifesting in the life of the disciple of Jesus.

"They profess that they know God; but in works they deny *him*, being abominable, and disobedient, and unto every good work reprobate." Titus 1:16

The danger of losing out with God may be harsh news to you. It is nonetheless biblically true. We must crucify emotions and live by divine truth; letting God be true and any other teaching or emotional feeling to be the liar (Rom. 3:3-4).

"Trust in the LORD with all thine heart; and lean not unto thine own understanding. In all thy ways acknowledge him, and he shall direct thy paths." Proverbs 3:5-6

The LORD told us to **"watch and pray that ye enter not into temptation"** and to **"exhort one another daily, while it is called To day; lest any of you be hardened through the deceitfulness of sin."** (Mathew 26:41; Hebrews

3:13) Also: **"...But exhorting *one another*: and so much the more, as ye see the day approaching. For if we sin wilfully after that we have received the knowledge of the truth, there remaineth no more sacrifice for sins, But a certain fearful looking for of judgment and fiery indignation, which shall devour the adversaries."** (Hebrews 10:25-27)

Do we not rather desire to abide in the place of blessing with our LORD? Do we not long to experience His hand of blessing upon our lives as we live in harmony with Him?

"If they obey and serve *him*, they shall spend their days in prosperity, and their years in pleasures." Job 36:11

"For he that soweth to his flesh shall of the flesh reap corruption; but he that soweth to the Spirit shall of the Spirit reap life everlasting. And let us not be weary in well doing: for in due season we shall reap, if we faint not." Galatians 6:8-9

Prayer: *Father, please keep me. Preserve my soul. Let me never be caught up with the deceit of many of those who claim to know You and yet have no fear of God before their eyes. Let me never be at ease in Zion/lukewarm lest I be spewed from Thy body/kingdom and rejected as a castaway/reprobate. In Jesus' name, amen.*

Chapter Eleven

"Abide in Me"

"I (Jesus) am the true vine, and my Father is the husbandman. Every branch in me that beareth not fruit he taketh away: and every branch that beareth fruit, he purgeth it, that it may bring forth more fruit. Now ye are clean through the word which I have spoken unto you. Abide in me, and I in you. As the

**branch cannot bear fruit of itself, except it
abide (remain) in the vine; no more can ye,
except ye abide in me. I am the vine, ye are
the branches: He that abideth in me, and I
in him, the same bringeth forth much fruit:
for <u>without me ye can do nothing</u>. <u>If a man
abide (remain) not in me, he is cast forth as
a branch, and is withered; and men gather
them, and cast them into the fire, and they
are burned</u>.” John 15:1-6**

As you can witness by the words of our LORD,
abiding or remaining in Him is essential. Those
who do not remain intimately in relationship
with Christ after He saves them, are in danger
of being **“cast ... into the fire, and ...
burned.”**

**There is Evidence in the Lives of all Who are
Truly Abiding in Christ**

Just after he detailed the 17 sinful works of the
flesh, the Holy Spirit gives us the nine dimen-
sions of the evidence of the LORD’s workings in

that person who is truly abiding in a saving relationship with Christ.

"But the fruit (evidence) of the Spirit is <u>love</u>, <u>joy</u>, <u>peace</u>, <u>longsuffering</u>, <u>gentleness</u>, <u>goodness</u>, <u>faith</u>, <u>Meekness</u>, <u>temperance</u>: against such there is no law." Galatians 5:22-23

The fruit of our lives testifies to who we are truly serving. It's a litmus test we can always read and monitor to see if we are truly in a saving relationship with Christ. Yielding to self or the Savior is a daily choice we must all make.

"Know ye not, that to whom ye yield yourselves servants to obey, his servants ye are to whom ye obey; whether of sin unto death, or of obedience unto righteousness?" Romans 6:16

Consider the following words from Romans 8:

"Therefore, brethren, we are debtors, not to the flesh, to live after the flesh. <u>For if ye live after the flesh, ye shall die: but if ye through</u>

the Spirit do mortify the deeds of the body,
ye shall live. For as many as are led by the
Spirit of God, they are the sons of God." Romans 8:12-14

Can you identify the divine promise in the following verse of Scripture?

"Know ye not that ye are the temple of God,
and *that* the Spirit of God dwelleth in you?
If any man defile the temple of God, him
shall God destroy; for the temple of God is
holy, which *temple* ye are." 1 Corinthians
3:16-17

The following is a divine command:

"Keep thyself pure." 1 Timothy 5:22

When we see sinful manifestations of the fallen
nature in our lives, we should recognize that
this reveals that our hearts are not presently in
a right relationship with the LORD. This is a
blessing to us from our LORD in that He gave
us exact knowledge of what He considers to be

sin, so that we never need to wonder, but can always have a measurement of where we are with Him.

"*This* I say then, Walk in the Spirit, and ye shall not fulfil the lust of the flesh. For the flesh lusteth against the Spirit, and the Spirit against the flesh: and these are contrary the one to the other: so that ye cannot do the things that ye would. But if ye be led of the Spirit, ye are not under the law." Galatians 5:16-18

Prayer: *LORD, Your Word alone is final authority. No other source compares. All others and other sources pale in comparison to You, the Most High God who gave us Your written Word. LORD, I repent of ever taking You for granted, not seeking You whole heartedly, and being negligent to study Thy Holy Precepts. Bless my heart to fear You severely and be moved into obedience as I look for the soon return of Jesus Christ, hastening in holy fear toward being pre-*

pared always to meet Him! In Jesus' name, amen.

Chapter Twelve

You can Have a ... A FRESH START WITH GOD

Jesus is the Great Shepherd of His Sheep (Heb. 13:20; Lk. 15)

This short look will help you get on track with the LORD, from where ever you may presently be. Take close heed to these words from your Maker and Savior and apply them directly to your life. This may very well be your last call and opportunity before it's too late.

"Seek ye the Lord while he may be found, call ye upon him while he is near: Let the wicked forsake his way, and the unrighteous man his thoughts: and let him return unto the Lord, and he will have mercy upon him; and to our God, for he will abundantly pardon." Isaiah 55:6-7

Acknowledge Your Sins

"Cast away from you all your transgressions, whereby ye have transgressed; and make you a new heart and a new spirit: for why will ye die, O house of Israel?" Ezekiel 18:31

The LORD is Abundantly Merciful but Only to those who Genuinely and Sincerely Repent and Turn Fully to Him

"A new heart also will I give you, and a new spirit will I put within you: and I will take away the stony heart out of your flesh, and I will give you an heart of flesh. And I will put

my spirit within you, and cause you to walk in my statutes, and ye shall keep my judgments, and do them." Ezekiel 36:26-27

New Creatures in Christ

"Therefore if any man *be* in Christ, *he is* a new creature: old things are passed away; behold, all things are become new. And all things *are* of God, who hath reconciled us to himself by Jesus Christ, and hath given to us the ministry of reconciliation." 2 Corinthians 5:17-18

Fresh Forgiveness

"Remembering mine affliction and my misery, the wormwood and the gall. My soul hath *them* still in remembrance, and is humbled in me. This I recall to my mind, therefore have I hope. *It is of* the LORD'S mercies that we are not consumed, because his compassions fail not. *They are* new every morning: great *is* thy faithfulness. The LORD *is* my portion, saith my soul; therefore will I

hope in him. The LORD *is* good unto them that wait for him, to the soul *that* seeketh him. *It is* good that *a man* should both hope and quietly wait for the salvation of the LORD." Lamentations 3:19-26

Fresh Oil

"But my horn shalt thou exalt like *the horn of* an unicorn: I shall be anointed with fresh oil." Psalms 92:10

Are you in need of a fresh beginning? The LORD specializes and delights in giving fresh, clear, and clean beginnings (Isaiah 54:7; 61:3; Ezekiel 36:36b; Luke 4:18; 15:1-31).

"To appoint unto them that mourn in Zion, to give unto them beauty for ashes, the oil of joy for mourning, the garment of praise for the spirit of heaviness; that they might be called trees of righteousness, the planting of the Lord, that he might be glorified." Isaiah 61:3

Are you genuinely open to and ready to hear and obey the truth in order to be blessed with a new beginning? If so, keep reading, open your whole heart, and get ready to be blessed.

1. Schedule God into your very first waking moments for prayer communion and the study of His Word (Ps. 5:3; 63:1; Mk. 1:35). He is the Cornerstone of your day and life.

2. Study God's Word diligently: Get blank index cards and get ready to begin capturing God's Word and memorizing it (Prov. 4:4, 21; Jn. 5:39; 2 Tim. 2:15). Carry those Scriptures on index cards where ever you go and read, meditate and memorize them. Feed on God's Word (1 Pet. 2:2).

3. Get a King James Bible and discard all artificial, supposedly "easy to understand" counterfeit, corrupt Bible versions. See "Bible Versions" page.

4. Confess, repent of, and forsake all known sins before the LORD, beginning with the sin of not placing the LORD first in your life (Exod. 20:3-4; Prov. 28:13; 1 Jn. 1:9).

5. Be resolved in the truth that you have been granted a whole new life and that you are not your own but the LORD's who bought you with His precious blood (Acts 20:28; 1 Cor. 6:19-20; 2 Cor. 5:17-18).

6. Die down deep into the death of Christ and learn what the daily cross truly is. Cease serving yourself and self-interests and serve only the LORD and others. Read 1 Corinthians 13 and Philippians 2:3-5 every day prayerfully.

7. Gain an eternal perspective about your brief life in this world as you walk with Jesus. Read Colossians 3:1-4 every day and pray over it.

8. Daily expect persecution, suffering, testings, and trials for the Word's sake (Mk. 4:17; 2 Tim. 3:12; James 1:2-4; 1 Pet. 4:12).

9. Communicate the Gospel of Jesus to others in every way that you possible can. Number your short days on this earth and redeem or buy back for lost time (Ps. 90:12; Eph. 5:16). Ask the LORD to make you fruitful in His eternal kingdom and that your fruit will remain (Ps. 2:8; Jn. 15:16).

10. Understand the biblical truth that you are commanded to fear God and you are *not* "once saved always saved." (Josh. 24:14; Ps. 2:11-12; Lk. 12:4-5) If you die in sin, the one true God and Judge of your eternal soul who is **"Holy, holy, holy,"** will send you irrevocably to hell (Hebrews 12:14; Revelation 2-3; 21:8, 27; 22:15).

Cry out to the LORD in prayer daily and moment by moment. Here are two stellar verses you will need to pray into your life daily:

"Create in me a clean heart, O God; and renew a right spirit within me." Psalms 51:10

"Unite my heart to fear thy name." Psalms 86:11

Sign up for the **Moments with My Master** email which is sent out 2-3 times weekly for the edification of the body of Christ. Go to Safe-GuardYourSoul.com to sign up or request by email at info@ SafeGuardYourSoul.com.

For a full study of this important topic and so much more, get the book titled *Lie of the Ages* available in e-book and print formats at SafeGuardYourSoul.com.

GOSPEL TRACTS Available

LOSER

Jesus told us all that only the losers will gain eternal life (Matt. 10:38-39). With the holy law to convict of sin, the necessity of "repentance toward God and faith toward our Lord Jesus Christ," and the holiness of our Maker emphasized, this Gospel tract has already blessed tens of thousands of souls with the knowledge of God. It's very well received among people. The ease of handing this one out is second to none. May God bless the conversations we are able to engage in when handing this one out to the lost and when supplying other Christians.

Read and Order Your Supply Today at SafeGuardYourSoul.com

Diary of a Dead Man

With the horrible cover image, this tract instantly grabs the attention of the recipient. While handing this one out, one may choose to ask, "That's a horrible image huh?" The person receiving the tract will then say, "Yes it sure is." To this the believer can respond with, "Please don't end up like that guy." This is also a very easy Gospel tract to distribute with wide receptivity – sure to make your seed sowing journey very fruitful.

Read and Order Your Supply Today at
SafeGuardYourSoul.com

JESUS: *Why Did This Man Die On A Cross?*

*With millions in print, the JESUS Tract is reaching thousands of lost souls globally and is perhaps the most condensed and complete presentation of the holy law and Gospel available in tract form today. This tract contains a glorious exaltation of the **"Great Shepherd of the sheep,"** the **"Good Shepherd"** who came to pay the complete price for the sins of His fallen creation (Heb. 13:20; Jn. 10:1-10). Order your supply today and begin using these messengers to reach those for whom He died and rose again.*

Read and Order Your Supply Today at SafeGuardYourSoul.com

SECRETS *From Beyond the Grave*

Shocking and thought-provoking secrets about the after-life. Contains a blistering menu of what awaits all who are not born again. This message is not for those who wish to hide the whole truth about eternal things. SE-CRETS is a tract few can resist reading with its aesthetic wickedness which reeks of death, and the curiosity pro-voking title. The message is 100% Gospel!

**Read and Order Your Supply Today at
SafeGuardYourSoul.com**

Order Your Supply of Soul Winning Gospel Tracts
Today at:

SafeGuardYourSoul.com

SafeGuardYourSoul

9201 Warren Parkway Suite 200

Frisco, TX 75035

469.334.7090

SHARPENING YOUR PERSONAL DISCERNMENT

For the Building Up of His Saints

To begin receiving the
Moments for My Master **email devotionals,
sign up at <u>SafeGuardYourSoul.com</u>**

Also, sign up for print newsletter on site.

Soul Damning Sins

Are there sins listed in God's Word that will damn one's soul to eternal hell? This is shocking revelation sure to strike the fear of God in the hearts of any who dare read this brief book. Great to read and to order copies to give away to others.

Find out more at www.SafeGuardYourSoul.com

ANOTHER BOOK FROM
SAFEGUARDYOURSOUL

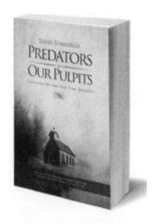

Predators in Our Pulpits
Invasion of the End Time Wolves

The prophesied great falling away is upon us – it's in our very "Christian" pulpits, books, and programs. As promised by our LORD and His apostles, "evil men and seducers" are waxing "worse and worse" in this late hour before our Savior's return (2 Tim. 3:13). Posing as ministers of righteousness, they have crept into the midst of biblically illiterate audiences on the wheels of their Trojan horse subterfuge and are promulgating poisonous pabulums in the pond of the heart of the people. These beguilers are depositing horrid heresies in the hearts of their hearers (1 Tim. 4:1-3).

Millions are becoming casualties of their war on the God of truth as they feverishly prey upon unlearned and unstable souls. Our only protection from the father of lies and his emissaries is to go deeper into the LORD ourselves, learning His truth and walking in the Holy Spirit. The contents of this volume will greatly enlighten the reader and direct his steps down the narrow road of light and truth, ever deepening His roots in the King of the soon coming, conquering and eternal kingdom of God .

What should the God-fearing do in response to this epidemic of evil that has invaded the modern church? How can we discern *who* and *what* teachings are true or false? Discover these answers in this timely, epic volume permeated with rarely revealed truth sure to nourish and sharpen any heart that hungers for more of Christ and His righteousness.

Find out more at www.SafeGuardYourSoul.com

ANOTHER BOOK FROM
SAFEGUARDYOURSOUL

Raised Up

This volume centers upon the essential cross and resurrection power of the Most High, raising upward the bowed down disciple who waits upon Him in fervent expectancy of His divine life and soon return.

The call of God upon every believer to die downward that He might raise them upward to fruitfulness in His life and power.

"And the remnant that is escaped of the house of Judah shall again take root downward, and bear fruit upward." Isaiah 37:31

Upward fruit bearing occurs as the disciple takes root downward, being buried down deeply into the death and burial of Christ. The One who is

"the resurrection, and the life" then simultane-
ously raises up that downward dying saint to
newness of life in His Spirit (Jn. 11:25; Rom.
8:11).

*Here is some of what you will learn in the pages of
this volume:*

- *How to sink down deep into the death and burial of
  Christ, that God might raise you upward to bear abundant fruit for His glory*
- *The importance of loving and honoring the LORD
  above self, and seeing His grace and power work in
  you in ministry to others*
- *How to discern which leaders are teaching the truth
  from the many wolves among us*
- *How to incorporate the cross in your personal life daily, and live a life fully pleasing to God*
- *The importance of prayer as you expectantly look for
  the soon and glorious return of the LORD Jesus Christ*

*In this poignant and timely volume, the person who is
possessed by a self-serving "What's in it for ME" mentali-
ty instead of "How can I most please my LORD Jesus," is
going to discover just how Luciferic his current views are.
It is hoped that he will then be brought to repentance and
a laying down of his life, that Christ alone might reign
(Isa. 14:12-15; James 4:6-10). Ready or not - Jesus is coming (Lk. 21:34-36). Are you ready?*

ANOTHER BOOK FROM
SAFEGUARDYOURSOUL

Deceivers and False Prophets Among Us

THE BOOK SOME LEADERS HOPE YOU NEVER FIND OUT ABOUT

Are there false, fruitless and even deceptive predators in the pulpits of the modern church? If so, are these deceivers leading multitudes to the worship of false gods through their damnable heresies? Are "seeker-friendly" churches creating a new class of "Christians" who have no concept of authentic, Biblical Christianity? Are there leaders who are building their own kingdoms in lieu of God's and doing so on your dime? Are we hearing the full-counsel of the LORD from those in leadership, or the psychology and programs of mere men? Are beguiling emissaries in our midst drawing believers away from pure devotion and intimacy with Jesus Christ? Do these things exist within your local fellowship? Are you truly being instructed in the right ways of the LORD? Explore the answers to these and many more questions in this bold, insightful, and resourceful look at the church world today.

WHAT YOU WILL GAIN FROM READING THIS BOOK:

o   What specific erroneous teachings are circulating in the church world and how to identify and expose them

o   How to discern the genuine leaders who truly follow the Word and Spirit of God, from the false and fruitless who are using God's money to build their own kingdoms

o   How to please the LORD by positioning and establishing His written revelation as final authority in your personal life

o   How to discern and cease wasting your brief existence on this earth supporting wolves in sheep's clothing

o   How to serve God with a loving and concerned heart from the foundation of divine immutable truth

278 Pages

Find out more at www.SafeGuardYourSoul.com